Kenneth Trimble

Fierce Light

Littlefox press

FIERCE LIGHT
Poetry
By Kenneth Trimble

Published by Littlefox Press
Postal address
PO Box 816 Kyneton
VIC 3444 Australia
At Alice & Co
7 High street Kyneton Vic 3444 Australia
www.aliceonhighstreet.com.au

Copyright © Kenneth Trimble 2016

ISBN 978-0-9925562-6-6

Cover artwork and cover design
by Sukhee Kwon
Copyright © Sukhee Kwon 2016

No part of this publication may be re-sold, hired out, reproduced, stored in a retrieval system or transmitted in any form or by any means without the prior written consent of the author and the publisher

*What was it like
when you were waiting to be born ...*

Foreword

Kavisha Mazzella AM

Ken Trimble' s poems express his inner and outer journeys through India, revealing his passion, his seeking of spirit and beauty – in temples and rooming houses and in a woman's arms and sweet yearning forever. His words speak of sacred tenderness and the fragility of life, inviting you to bite deep into its juicy flesh. At times, he is a little brother of the Dharma Bums or a cousin of Zorba, at other times, the child of Buddha and Kali. In any case he's showing up uninvited, knocking on your door after some wine or coffee depending on if he's giving it up for Lent or not. The poetic incantation might go until dawn, and he will crash out on your living room floor…are you ready to receive this guest? Ken brings dignity and consciousness to his pain and lifts it up transformed; he's a rebel against a life of indifference, seeking beauty in inner understanding.

Fierce light

Black hymns I.

There was a time father
when you loved me.

You wrote my name down
on your pillow at night.

You told me your bedtime
stories without a yawn

and you sang my song
before the dawn.

Father, I remember your
six o'clock swill and you falling
pissed into the cat tray at night.

You took me to your place of work,
a newspaper, feral on the ink, with a
smell that got lost in your veins

And our birthdays were
on the same day and month.

When I was twenty- one
You were fifty.

We were Librans circling each
other like distant planets on the run.

And mercy's hand you held out to me
all those moons ago

when I was so busy
being young.

There was a time father
when you loved me,

you didn't need a Bible,
no words of wisdom

from God's holy mouth,
the dark star of your hopes,

I was your sweet pagan
child running wild.

Oh father, there was a time
when you loved me, and I will

sing my black hymn to you,
till we meet by the edge of light.

Black hymns II

Some say that first cry
as you come out of your
Mother's womb is the cry
of the Universe being born

Yet the deepest cry
came at the foot of my
Mother's corpse.

Amen friend.
Amen light.

Fierce light

Gods and monsters rage inside my head
like a turpentine drunk
as an orphaned yellow moon drinks illuminations

to my medicated night -

You were right when you told me life is a paradox
between saints and degenerates.

These visions came out of the blue
no peyote or magic mushrooms,
my mind split as if by lighting
piercing this self I no longer knew.

My soul shattered in two crying gibberish
into the new dawn with a
fierce light burning away my false image
as the whole world screamed.

Oh brief, exquisite, holy gone moment,
alive and dying-death and rebirth-a continual movement,

a never-ending circle-whole Cosmoses
born and destroyed,
multiple universes exploded before my eyes-supernovas,

whole constellations of new flowering frontiers,
and I, well I had disappeared into THAT,
and the heartbeat I heard was the heartbeat of the world.

Sweet revelation I was no longer separate and my body
had turned into a weight of holy water with my head
exploding

into fragments of divine wyrdness and my soul became an
uncaged bird flying high above the

firmament of my feverish mind,
and as I stood there I knew
I was forgiven – forgiven
for every goddamn thing I ever did,

forgiven for daring to think I even mattered,
I had no more currency than a Wall Street crash

worthless I was free to roam, no longer was I chained
to this wheel of constant becoming, and became in an
instant, my wounded angel's grace.

Murders, mountains, and poems

Kalighat devotees pray to the Goddess,
nights of ecstasy follow me down,
singing sad eyed lady.

I wish I were crazy wild instead of crazy,
wild enough to pump heroin, to feel the
white lady of Sudder Street pimps.

Two transvestites kiss lightly, laughing
with betel juice smiles, while transactions
are made at the Blue Sky Café.

I hobble to the Fairlawn Hotel with taunts from
street urchins,

'be careful uncle, be careful'.

I was bought up never to show my feelings,
to be vulnerable was weak.

I never hugged my father, our hands were
cold as a Warburton winter.

Boys don't cry.
Men don't cry.

I drink my memory with a limp, and back
home waits the Gatwick, jazz, and rooming house
murders with songs, and poems.

Constant rain

India has seeped into my skin like constant rain.
I am a monsoon man where
all about me is constant sorrow, and sometimes joy.
The beggar and the Brahmin. The holy and the fake.
The real and the unreal.
Here illusion rains into reality as storm surges into light.
Time a meaningless word.
A memory present is already the

Past.

A face glaring in the mirror.
A woman pleads in the slum.
A walk under Tamil stars
With a holy man.

And a beggar with no eyes and hands
calls out prayers of poverty
on to the fingertips of his lost angels.
His footpath a call to life, and the dangerous rain, a call
to life, for what else is there, but life,
because to roll over is not an option.

Nobody escapes.
Here everybody shits in the same river,
rich or poor.

My LSD is in my chai, it strokes my wild hair.
I can leave anytime I want that's a truth not denied,
go back to suburbia, get my dole check,
drink my life away,
but India never leaves me,
for I am stuck inside her web, sold, souled,
and stroked.

6 pm

Peacocks stir in evening light.
Hush – old man sways to the rhythm
of Shiva Arunachala.
I turn to the west.
Hush –
A thousand bodies lay like prayers
before me. Shiva dancing
on a mountain.
Old Ramana smiling. Hidden,
his body everybody.
I hear the footsteps.
Hush!

The divine comic

God is a shaman turning tricks,
an eagle dissolving into fish.

A fish dissolving into stone.
A stone dissolving into mountain.

A mountain dissolving into lake.
A lake dissolving into sky.

A sky dissolving into sea.
A sea dissolving into man.

A man dissolving into woman.
A woman dissolving into earth.

An Earth dissolving into river.
A river dissolving into Buddha.

A Buddha dissolving into Jesus.
A Jesus dissolving into Shams.

A Shams dissolving into madness.
A madness dissolving into truth.

A truth dissolving into lies.
A lie dissolving into silence.

A silence dissolving into Om.
An Om dissolving into body.

A body dissolving into space,
and all around us laughter

dissolving into laughter
as the divine comic plays his

Chaplin to us while we hope against hope,
actors playing roles that God stole.

Goddess

Praying in the temple
with you by my side
I wasn't thinking of prayers to God but to you.
Eternal beauty
if you had taken off your clothes
I would have made love to you right there
in front of
Jesus.

Snow falling among the pines

Dogs fly in the night.
Buddhist monks walk on air,
tea in a bowl,
I bow to the bow.

Wild West town
without the cowboys.

The Oracle has gone on holidays.
The Dalai Lama is in recess.
Prayer wheel spinning the world.

Himalayan pines tingle with snow
as the Abbot gives silk scarf, an
old Buddha with toothless smile.

Snow falling
full moon dreaming on a
quiet wind.

Kundun is playing in town
while a young boy sleeps to
Philip Glass.

Young monks watch
as I am accosted by growling mastiff-
be patient friend.

Footsteps enter the monastery
my soul comes in next.
Prayer begins.

A genius of God

Meditation in the Guru's hut 4am.

Torchlight guides me along the jungle path.
Old man greets me with 'Jesus is coming for you'.

6am bell tolls for prayer.

I stagger covered by mosquito repellent.
Head to foot-my shawl covers me like a monk.
I sit cross-legged to Christ/ Buddha in the cave.

Here no beat madness.
No curving of time to something I never was.
No worship at the altar of hip.

I sit with my sanyassin friend
his eyes are founts of light.

A divine cadence sings his mysterious spirit.

No need to speak- no brag-
he was a genius of God.

I'll buy you a bunch of red roses

Kashi, city of light –
Great Ganga explodes with people
praying day and night.

Lunatic Linga cries as women pour
milk over the black, formless, form.

Ash lingers on the nostril.

River of skulls
float into the Dark Mother of eternity.

They say when they opened
Kabir's coffin they found
a bunch of red roses.

The footsteps of God lead
to the river.

Kabir is everywhere!

I am caught by the spiritual
overload of Shakti frenzy.

I hear a girl talk of Khajuraho
and tantric gymnastics.

People are bewitched
by this icon of light.

Madness a familiar smell
as I haunt the Ghats.

And the fire keeps burning.
It goes on, forever.

Bob Dylan, the beggar, and the lost

A contorted body crying out begs with open palm
as my eyes stare in terror.

I flee from my own darkness a Charlie Chaplin
hopping away from pain.

I've got Dylan in my backpack
my constant companion

through the hells of Kolkata streets.
I fumble with love minus zero

chanting it like a Brahmin priest
while I ripped the plaster from my shattered leg.

I sat and cried in unison with the beggar
a face I could not see.

Her old milk crate bed

We wore pork pie hats.
We listened to Patti Smith rage.
We made love on your
old milk crate bed.

My blood in your veins.

I bought you a book of
love poems
by Neruda.

You gave me your mouth
bending into morning

my tongue trailed
along your back,
you quivering

in the soft light.

We talked about India.
We talked about Rishikesh.

I told her she should see
the sun rise
over the Ganges

it is amazing.

I wrote you a poem
you posted it on
your wall.

A turning of the heart

It was a turning of the heart that
changed me.

I turned around and saw myself
perhaps for a minute.

A moment distilled in all other moments.

It came and it went, it came and it went
with each breath/ each breath/ each breath/
each breath.

Clouds coming /clouds going/clouds no more/
One falls. One gets up.

And the greater the fall the greater
the glimpse.

Temple of Venus

If I was Neruda
I would kiss your sweet rose

If I was Borges
I would paint your imagination

If I was Lorca
I would celebrate your body

But I am none of these
just a simple poet

who dreams of a girl
in a distant land

where eagles fly over the Yucatan
and ayahuasca is swallowed in iquitos

looking for that perfect Yage
the perfect Blake to enter
your doors

I lay down

I feel the nakedness of your tree
as your branches hold my name.

Scratching my chest you
make me bleed as I feel the blow
of your foreign land.

I lay down among your moist
Earth and kiss your leaves
that cushions my soul.

My fingers caress the page with
my pen as I etch your name.

Blessings

Tripping to Earth's sounds and wonder
I have glimpsed eternity and felt its silent roar.

I have heard a tree sing on my evening
stroll downtown.

I have felt the invisible hand of a child
touch my crazy wanderlust soul.

I have smelled death in the living on the hair of
my Benedictus girl.

I have placed a candle via an old Babushka's
hand as the Berlin Wall fell.

I have heard the call to prayer from a
haunted desert crying while my mother lay
slowly dying.

I have felt the whisper in my ear, 'don't worry',
while around me War.

I have danced in Zikr chanting Allah Hu as the
waves crashed wild on the sundown shore.

I have chanted the psalms before the frosted
Dawn.

I have seen a Buddhist monk bow in blessing
on a calm summer's day and felt the rage of
God humble and break me yet more.

Now

I move more slowly to catch these
precious calls.

Conversation with a God

I was sixteen when I saw the film Woodstock. It was at the Palladium that later became a car park. There were three acts that impressed me – Crosby, Stills, & Nash, Joe Cocker, and Richie Havens. When I saw Havens it was like listening to God. I was hooked and I bought all his albums. Fast-forward thirty-four years. A friend I met in India with two others started up an arts magazine called Troika. Over a beer one night he asked if I would like to interview Richie Havens on a phone hook up via Carlton & New York. He knew I loved him. It was like a gift from the Gods. I was just a poor working class boy from the western suburbs, and my life was as far removed from rock n roll as the Earth from the Moon. After smoking close to a pack of cigarettes in two hours, finally, I got the nerve to interview him. What transpired was forty-five minutes of generosity I'll never forget. He told me he played for three hours. They couldn't get the acts in because of the weather, and the traffic jam. It was brilliant. I told him a story I heard from Woody Guthrie. It goes like this-Papa rabbit & Mama rabbit were playing in a field when they heard the sounds of hunting dogs. The two rabbits ran into a hollow log trembling as the dogs sniffed around the entrance. Mama rabbit said to Papa rabbit, "well then, what do we do now"? Papa rabbit thought for a moment, "well, we'll just stay here till we out number them". Havens laughed like crazy. It was the best time of my life. The magazine closed down. I never did get to see Havens. And when I heard he passed away, I felt real sad. He was a nice guy. After the interview I went back to reality working in Aged Care. Ah, such is life!

A country road

To walk a country road
and be held captive by a flower
that's beauty in its purest form.

An ordinary moment open to all
and once you've smelled
that perfume rising from its
loving cup
you are forever changed.

Its like you no longer know
where you are
or who you're supposed to be.

It's as if you are caught between
two worlds.

October moon

Awake at the
watchman's hour
to singing outside
my bedroom
window.

Nightingales?

I thought we had none.

This night had been
consummated
by angels.

I can feel your smirk
your intelligent justification
by too much reason.

No, I wasn't drinking.

Beyond my bedroom
Window two angels
came to set me
free

because the
sounds they
made was not
of this Earth.

The midnight sun
came down to Earth
that night and sang
me a lullaby.

It was my
Monastic call
to be.

Before India
Before Bede.

And I felt myself being
reshaped into something
new.

And the October moon
was smiling as the rest
of the world slept

while I sat and listened
to my celestial duet.

Were they nightingales?

Who cares.

Dancing with myself

I woke up that morning
speaking in a foreign tongue,
weird feelings overcame me.

I began speaking in Pali
reciting some ancient Buddhist text-

My teacher said these things
are just sensations

let them go!

But I was convinced I had entered
into a new world

a world I knew so well

and these men who walked around me
damn it I know them!

In the evening I sat down on the
trampled grass
and watched the mountains.

Light was turning into dark while
silence was emerging out of sound

while

I reached out and touched those
mountains with my hand.

God said hey, don't worry,
it's real friend.

Come, dance with me.

The devious angel

Hold me morning sun, caress the aches and pains
from my night, allow the child to enter my soul,
allow the light to guide me on, without this ghostly
fright.

Hold me morning sun, when night and day
are same, a gift given, only a devious angel
could gain.

Hold me morning sun, through my stormy dreams,
for its one step on, and two steps back, on this
my wilderness track.

Hold me morning sun, delight my heart with your
ancient wisdom's call, a shining path this light,
leading me on, this my wild, lonesome night.

Hold me morning sun, your spirit that dwell
in me Awake, awake, the day has
finally come!

What was it like...

What was it like when
you were waiting to be born.
Was it dark and wet.
Was there light in there.
Did you hear voices.
Sounds of lovemaking.
A sound of birds.
Sounds of anger.
Did you hear laughter.
Did you feel pain.
Did the moon speak to you
while you lay curled.
Did you dream of sand
mountains, flowering stones,
and skies of fire.
Did you hear the prayer
of an old monk singing
your soul.
Did you touch sadness.
Did you touch the heart
that beats
when you are caught by
the wings of love, or was
there doubt.
What was it like when

you were waiting to be born.
Did the clouds call your name?

Butterflies in her hair

I knew a woman who carried all the butterflies
of Canada in her hair.

She would dance naked in the forest, a nymph,
without any notion of sin.

She drew a circle in the dirt,
and sat down on the earth for
four days and nights,
chanting a new world into existence.

The butterflies made her glow like a beacon of light,
giving succour to the needy.

The people in the area called her the
Butterfly Lady of Compassion.

And the sun smiled and the moon danced.
And the night was full of crazy Vincent lost in Arles.

I knew a woman who carried all the butterflies
of Canada in her hair.

And I sit here in W Tree chanting verse to
Goddess Tara before the always – new dawn.

Peace comes by waiting

Mahabalipuram beer in a teapot sand
dynasty washed by the sea.
Pretty girl sways her hips to a sixties
psychedelic rave party going on.

Half-way point to my ashram –

Long way from Krishnamurti on
Adyar wanderings under the banyan tree
reading freedom from the known

listening to the Imam's call to prayer
in the dying light.

An old woman whispered in my ear,
'can you feel the sacredness here'?
I felt my soul leap/ recognition perhaps?

Shantivanam my forest of peace-

Here in my tiny hut I sit with my
creature friends, fireflies, sparkle above
my mosquito net – spiders cling
like trapeze artists as
bats hug the walls.

Later I dig a well for Yesudas laughing
in the mud and water with
my Yogananda man.

In the morning light

Sanyassins arrive by bullock cart
wearing their robe of the dead.

Tell Myles I sent you

I was staying at the Adelaide Hostel in Isadora Duncan Lane, San Francisco. A fellow I met there said, 'lets have a drink down near the Tenderloin District', famous in the old days for its butcher ways. In a bar as dark as midnight, the owner said, 'go down to Green Street to O'Reilly's, and say hello to Myles the owner. I'll tell him you're coming. Go on Irish night'. It was on Green Street near Columbus Avenue, and Kerouac paradise. I arrived around 8 o'clock, and said to the barmaid, 'is Myles around?' The place came alive as people crowded in. The barman was serving beers and playing his fiddle at the same time. The joint was jumping. Myles said, 'put your money in your pocket, the beers are on the house'. People came up to me and said, 'you're that Australian poet'. I met a fellow who knew Ramblin' Jack Elliott, and Gurdjieff's great grandson. A girl quoted 'writing down the bones'. The night rolled on like a carousel as I drank to Jack, Allen, Corso, Burroughs, Snyder, and every other fucker. By the end, the band played Waltzing Matilda, and I sang like a wounded bear as the night waned into morning. Yes Australians, head to O'Reilly's, and tell Myles I sent you.

Okay

To be vulnerable
is beautiful.

To fall down
is beautiful.

To get off your
knees is beautiful.

For you need to eat
dirt to appreciate the

Earth for in the end
and there's always
an end

only madmen see.

Satori night with Thomas Merton

A cliff hanging bus ride to Dharmasala by night.
Up the mountain without fear of the abyss. My soul,
mind, and body, unhinged by the unsettling

darkness.

Tibetans laugh, covered by thick winter gear,
I have only my South Indian shawl.
My limbs are chattering from the cold, or is it fear?

Milarepa snores in the back seat.

I am with an old man, a mystic, his eyes have that
far off look, as if they are seeing into some
magic, heavenly realm.

Buddha baby crying as

we talked about Thomas Merton, and how he
became Zen Merton, as well as Christ Merton.
We talked about his enlightenment at the foot of

the Buddha, and his death that came swift-
satori and death appropriate, one glimpse of
God then gone.

My friend has eyes of compassion,
I like his soul,
in the night we survive by telling stories of India.

By morning, we arrived in Dharmasala to monks
playing catch in the snow, and all around
the tall pines breathed high,

Himachel light

The caves at Ellore

I left the group
and stumbled
into a cave
a perfect womb shrouded
in prayer.

Eons of time had
developed this
shaman's rock
hidden from
religion.

No thought existed
A hundred million years ago.
No Buddha. No Christ. No Kali.
Only the dance of
darkness inside a
spark.

There were no morals
or ethics on sin.

No Genesis.

No mandala entry
points to God.

I was alone. There
was no world.
My breath breathed
Aum.

My body shook
disappearing into
a porthole of
new beginnings.

Cloud over my face

Cloud over my face
strokes my mouth
with poems not
written.

Sun strikes the
cloud as I strike
the light.

I count the years.
I count the years.

Cloud over my face
disappears in the rain.

Mirrors of reality

I look into your eye and I see me.
How can I say I love God if I fight
you every day.

Life is too short for such
childish nonsense.

I look into your eye and I see me
as you see you in me.

We are mirrors to this reality
as it was given by the Gods
which isn't much.

How can I discern the tiniest atom
for it's a matter of trust that I believe.

For without this I am nothing but
an empty shell.

Behind the veil

Christian prayer
in a Hindu world
on a sea of shit.

Mary and Kali
two faces of
the divine
virginal and
wild.

I see the outline
of her body
through the
veiled curtain.

I sat and watched
in silence as she
faced the other
way.

The curve of her hips
and arse so perfect
in the Indian light.

So beautiful are you
Goddess even God
might be tempted.

Tonight we will pray
in the big white church
and I shall watch

you in secret my
beautiful desire.

Song of the forest

A long walk in the forest
with friends.

Small talk with holy people.

People I have forgotten.

The fog has settled in and
all around me invisible beings
begin to whisper.

The primeval woods are
alive with the presence
of spirit.

I wrap my arms around this old
Tree called Ada and feel
her warmth.

Everything here is familiar,
old souls stand tall in the light.
Lyrebirds dance balletic
appearing as if in a dream.

There are songs in the

forest that are mysterious
that only an ancient heart could
understand.

Home-

I meditate in the chapel,
outside I hear river-sounds
and inside I hear the call to
prayer.

Path

Towards the mountains
God sent me
to re-discover beauty away from
stone, blood, and fear.

Towards life away from death.
Towards the ever beginning.

Here everything shines-

The LEAF and the ROCK.
The SILENCE and the WIND.

No religion/No dogma
disturbs my quiet walk.

Here is my church
everything on this path
a prayer.

Green hills of W Tree

There in hills
so precious green
I sit covered by white
shawl while morning
is still night with stars
so plentiful and close
I could gather them
with my hand.

And if you listen
closely you can
hear the corroboree
frogs chanting along
the Snowy mist.

Cold, I settle into
my posture.

And a light upon
light holds the
world while others
in the valley sleep.

What brilliance life
can bring away from
cynicism and fear.

Offering of light

We drove to the mountain with
his ashes in a shoebox by my side.
It was perfect as the sun began
to fade in the winter light.

We climbed the platform
and down below
Phillip Glass's
'Offering' rang out.

It was perfect as perfect is,
and when we got to the top,
I recited that poem from Clouds,
The one you thought you wrote,

You can never go home…

My friend tipped the ashes
and they shimmered
like curtains one after
the other.

And the light was ever
so small. A spark of
life for the approaching
night.

Acknowledgements

I wish to thank American artist Sukhee Kwon for the cover and Kavisha Mazzella for her foreword.

Other thanks are to Christine Mathieu my publisher and friend who has always supported me. Kris Hemensley and Retta from Collected Works. And the many poets who have helped and encouraged me over the years, and I guess some who may not even want these thanks but here goes: Robert Lloyd, Joe Bottone, Valli Poole, Karl Gallagher, Catfish McDaris, Mike Castro, L, and others, thanks also for George Harrison's song, My Sweet Lord

Lastly if it wasn't for my knockabout friend Gary who passed away from pancreatic cancer I doubt that any of this would have happened. The poem 'Offering' is for him.

Works by Kenneth Trimble

Clouds on Hanover Street
Shores of American Memory
The Barking Mad poems
the ghost to his green/a tribute to Dylan Thomas
with Littlefox Press, Australia

Dearth & Redemption by OpPress
with www.ISSUU.com USA
Drinking wine under the moon
with www.tenpagespress.com. USA

Works in American literary magazines
The Blue Hour, Gutter Eloquence, The Blue Lake Review.

www.Ijagunpoetryjournal.com Nigeria;
www.ColdnoonTravelPoetics New Delhi, India,
www.CUIB-NEST-NIDO.com
Revistă–Internaţională De Cultură Europe and Romania

Poems in Anthologies:
Fierce Invalids on the poet Rimbaud by Blind Dog Press. The Art of Being Human (Volume 1) by Brian Wrixon Books and The Frankston Writers Block and Opus Bound Text/Ures by OpPress.

The late Rhonda Jankovic on 3CR has interviewed Ken, and his work has been played on American Public Radio by Newamba Flamingo and by American poet Belinda Subramanian.

In Australia, Ken's work has appeared in:
www.collectedworks-poetryideasblogspot.com
www.desolationangels.com
Deakin University's poetry journal Windmill (red issue) and in www.horrorsleazetrash.com

Kenneth Trimble has been nominated three times for the prestigious American award 'The Pushcart Prize' founded by Paul Bowles and Anais Nin.

Ken has performed in many of Melbourne's poetry venues and was invited to read his work at the inaugural Newcastle Writers Festival and the Geelong Polyglot Festival. He has also performed in poetry venues in San Francisco and New Orleans.

Ken lived for some years in Warburton in Victoria's Yarra Valley where he was involved in a thousand year old Benedictine Community called the Camaldolese, a hermit order. He now lives in W Tree at the foot of the Snowy in a Buddhist community called SIBA.

He has travelled widely including four times to India where he visited pilgrimage sites; then China, Russia, Egypt, Ireland, Europe and America.

www.ingramcontent.com/pod-product-compliance
Lightning Source LLC
Chambersburg PA
CBHW062122080426
42734CB00012B/2951